our
Environment

Garbage

Karen D. Povey

KIDHAVEN PRESS
An imprint of Thomson Gale, a part of The Thomson Corporation

Detroit • New York • San Francisco • San Diego • New Haven, Conn.
Waterville, Maine • London • Munich

For more information, contact
KidHaven Press
27500 Drake Rd.
Farmington Hills, MI 48331-3535
Or you can visit our Internet site at http://www.gale.com

Picture credits: Cover photo: Altrendo Nature/Getty Images; © Mark Bolton/CORBIS, 28; © Ashley Cooper/CORBIS, 7; © david sanger photography/Alamy, 39; © Shelley Eades/San Francisco Chronicles/CORBIS, 42; © Kevin Fleming/CORBIS, 20 (large photo); © Todd Gipstein/CORBIS, 36; © James Leynse/CORBIS, 20 (inset); © Sally A. Morgan/Ecoscene/CORIBS, 23; PhotoDisc, 13 (inset), 32 (both photos); Photos.com, 6; PhotoSpin, 9; © Keith Pritchard/Boating Images Photo Library /Alamy, 8;© Louie Psihoyos/CORBIS, 19, 25; © Joel W. Rogers/CORBIS, 13 (large photo); © Skycam/CORBIS, 17; © Joseph Sohm/Chromo Sohm/CORBIS, 40; © Swerve/Alamy, 14; © Gari Wyn Williams/Alamy, 5

LIBRARY OF CONGRESS CATALOGING-IN-PUBLICATION DATA

Povey, Karen D., 1962-
Garbage / by Karen D. Povey.
p. cm. -- (Our environment)
Includes bibliographical references and index.
Contents: Too much trash—Where does garbage go?—Is recycling effective?—Reducing garbage.
ISBN 0-7377-3558-9 (hard cover : alk. paper) 1. Refuse and refuse disposal—Juvenile literature. I. Title. II. Series.
TD792.P69 2006
628.4'4--dc22   2006004170

contents

chapter one

Too Much Trash

People today produce a great deal of garbage. In the United States alone, nearly 240 million tons (218 million metric tons) of trash are created every year. The biggest problem with garbage is that once it is created, it never really goes away. Instead, garbage remains in the environment for a very long time, where it may cause harm to both people and wildlife.

The Dangers of Garbage

Some trash is purposely tossed or dumped into the environment. This garbage becomes **pollution** that fouls rivers, litters roadsides, and dirties sidewalks all over the world. Garbage is not only ugly, it can also be dangerous. Some garbage, such as paint cans, batteries, and discarded cleaning products, contains harmful chemicals called **toxins** that poison the air and water. Other garbage, such as plastic bags and food wrappers, may injure or kill wildlife that eat it. Broken glass and medical waste from hospitals can injure people and carry disease.

A discarded armchair sits alongside a road, part of the millions of tons of trash produced each year in the United States.

Litter is a problem all over the world. In Toronto, for example, nearly $16 million is spent picking up trash on the streets each year. Worldwide, the most common single type of litter is the cigarette butt. It is estimated that several trillion cigarette butts are thrown onto streets, sidewalks, and beaches every year. A cigarette butt contains traces of poisonous chemicals and a plastic filter that can be deadly to animals that eat it. Although each cigarette butt is small, taken together they add up to a huge garbage problem.

Cigarette butts are the most common form of trash worldwide.

An Ocean of Trash

One place where garbage often ends up is in the ocean. Garbage enters the ocean when it is washed from land through storm drains or dumped from ships. Each year nearly 15 billion pounds (6.8 billion kg) of trash is dumped from cruise ships, freighters, fishing boats, and recreational vessels. This ocean garbage drifts on currents to reach even islands thousands of miles from any continent. One scientist counted 950 pieces of trash, including plastic containers, bottles, ropes, and lightbulbs, along one small stretch of beach on a remote island in the South Pacific.

Some ocean garbage, such as paper, wood, and food waste, rots in a fairly short time. However, much of the garbage is made from materials that

Beachgoers in Spain relax on a garbage-strewn beach.

A dolphin that may have died of starvation after swallowing a plastic bag is washed up on the shore of an English beach.

Animals that become entangled in plastic six-pack rings could die from starvation or injuries.

do not easily break down, or **decompose**. This garbage includes glass bottles, metal cans, and plastic. Scientists estimate that plastic trash floating in the ocean may last up to 450 years. Plastic trash is especially dangerous for wildlife. Plastic bags and Styrofoam pieces are often mistaken for food by sea turtles and seabirds. Whales, dolphins, and sea turtles have been known to die after eating plastic bags that block the passage of food. Seabirds may mistake small plastic pieces for fish eggs. They feed their young this trash, and the chicks sometimes starve to death because their stomachs become filled with plastic and have no room for food.

Many ocean animals are harmed not by eating plastic but by becoming tangled in it. Seals sometimes catch their necks or flippers in plastic six-pack rings and slowly die from starvation or infected wounds. Discarded fishing line wraps around the legs of seabirds, causing injury or snagging on tree limbs. Lost fishing nets trap and

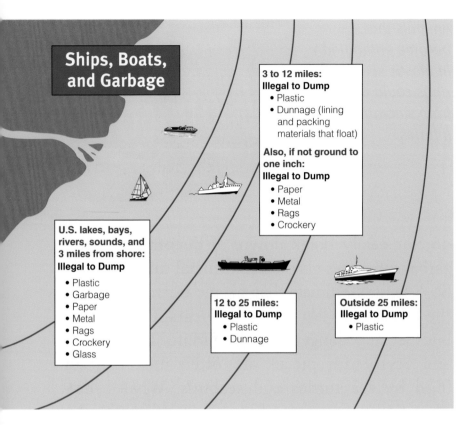

Ships, Boats, and Garbage

3 to 12 miles:
Illegal to Dump
- Plastic
- Dunnage (lining and packing materials that float)

Also, if not ground to one inch:
Illegal to Dump
- Paper
- Metal
- Rags
- Crockery

U.S. lakes, bays, rivers, sounds, and 3 miles from shore:
Illegal to Dump
- Plastic
- Garbage
- Paper
- Metal
- Rags
- Crockery
- Glass

12 to 25 miles:
Illegal to Dump
- Plastic
- Dunnage

Outside 25 miles:
Illegal to Dump
- Plastic

drown countless sharks, seals, whales, turtles, and birds every year.

Because garbage causes so much harm to marine wildlife, international laws have been passed to limit dumping in oceans. Since 1988, it has been illegal for ships to dump any plastic materials overboard. However, these laws are nearly impossible to enforce far out at sea, so dumping likely continues.

Trash Trends

Not all garbage ends up littering the environment. Most people throw their trash into garbage cans to be collected for disposal. Much of this collected garbage is buried in **landfills**. In a landfill, huge piles of trash are packed tightly together and covered with soil. Because little oxygen and water reaches this trash, it decomposes very slowly. As a result, the buried garbage will remain in the landfill for hundreds of years. Since people produce garbage much more quickly than nature can break it down, new and larger landfills are constantly needed.

Although modern landfills have been used only during the last several decades, people have always produced garbage. Studies of ancient civilizations show that people piled broken pottery and tools in trash piles thousands of years ago. Today, however, people create greater amounts and different types of garbage than people did in the past. Since 1960, the amount of garbage produced in the United States has more than doubled. Some of this increase is a result of the country's growing population—more people create more trash.

Personal Trash

Also increasing is the amount of trash each person produces. In 1960, the average American threw away less than 3 pounds (1.4kg) of trash each day. By 2003, the total had reached 4.5 pounds (2kg) per person. This increase is mostly the result of people's changing lifestyles. Because many people today are very busy with work and family activities, they often buy products that are packaged in ways that make them quicker and easier to use. Today's packages have handles, spouts, and other convenience gadgets built in. These gadgets create more packaging that ends up in the garbage. In addition, products once sold with little packaging, such as vegetables, juice, and meat, are now commonly sold wrapped in plastic or boxed in single-serving containers. People often buy heavily packaged convenience food such as microwavable dinners or meals from fast-food restaurants. In fact, packaging such as cans, jars, bottles, and boxes now makes up about one-third of all garbage buried in landfills.

Another change from several decades ago is that many products are now designed to be **disposable**, or thrown away after use. Tissues, paper plates, plastic razors, and foil baking pans have replaced longer-lasting products for many people. Even products designed to have a long life span, such as appliances and electronics, are often thrown away in favor of newer models.

High-Tech Trash

Some of the most commonly discarded products are cell phones and computer equipment. Technology advances quickly, making these products smaller and faster. As a result, electronic equipment often becomes outdated within just a few years of purchase. This outdated equipment, known as **e-waste**, has become the world's

A bulldozer (inset) is needed to compress garbage together to make the huge mounds found in landfills.

Discarded electronic equipment, like this cell phone, contains toxic materials that can poison the environment.

fastest-growing type of garbage. Each year 40 to 50 million cell phones are discarded in North America alone. Studies predict that 500 million personal computers will be discarded in the United States by 2007. Most of these will be buried in landfills. This high-tech trash contains toxic materials such as lead, mercury, and cadmium, which can poison the environment if not handled carefully.

Wasted Resources

In addition to taking up so much space in landfills and causing harmful pollution, garbage has another impact on the environment that most people never realize. It takes a huge amount of water, energy, and raw materials to make, package, and transport the products people buy. The trash people throw away is only a fraction of the actual garbage produced. In fact, it is estimated that for every 100 pounds (45kg) of products purchased, another 3,200 pounds (1,450kg) of waste are produced. If the amount of garbage thrown away continues to grow, there is the possibility that many natural resources will be used up faster than they can be replaced.

chapter two

Where Does Garbage Go?

Most people stop thinking about their trash when the garbage truck pulls away from the curb. But when garbage is thrown away, it does not disappear. Instead, it only moves out of sight. How garbage is handled after it is collected can determine its impact on the environment.

Going to the Dump

For hundreds of years, people have used garbage dumps to get rid of their trash. These dumps were usually fields and swamps on the outskirts of towns where people simply piled up their garbage. Left uncovered, the rotting trash smelled terrible, attracted rats, and spread disease. As cities grew and the amount of trash in dumps increased, the mess and odor eventually became unbearable. By the late 1930s, government officials started looking for other ways to deal with their growing mountains of garbage. They began to replace open dumps with landfills, where the waste was covered by a layer of dirt each day in an effort to control pests and odor.

By the 1950s, there were hundreds of landfills in use around the world. From the outside, these landfills looked much cleaner than open dumps,

A huge truck dumps garbage at a landfill in England as bulldozers pile the trash into mounds.

but they still had serious problems. Rainwater falling on the landfills became polluted by chemicals as it seeped through the rotting trash. This process created a thick toxic fluid called **leachate** that oozed out of the landfill. The leachate poisoned groundwater used for drinking and made its way into countless waterways. By the early 1990s, the government began taking steps to protect the environment by closing down these leaking landfills.

Fresh Kills Landfill

Before it closed in 2001, Fresh Kills Landfill in Staten Island, New York, was the world's largest landfill. Covering over 2,200 acres (89 hectares), Fresh Kills was the daily dumping ground for 16,000 tons (14,500 metric tons) of New York City's garbage for 50 years. Its large size and its setting in the midst of a marsh made Fresh Kills one of the world's most polluting landfills. Because Fresh Kills is built on marshland, water from streams and the changing tides is able to enter it and freely mix with the garbage inside. This creates rivers of toxic leachate that contaminate the groundwater beneath the landfill with a wide variety of dangerous chemicals. Leachate also makes its way into the wetlands and harbor surrounding the site, poisoning shellfish and other wildlife. Three million gallons (11.4 million liters) of leachate used to flow from the site daily. Today, much of the leachate is captured by a special system installed by order of the U.S. Environmental

Seagulls in search of food circle mounds of trash at Staten Island's Fresh Kills Landfill, the world's largest landfill until it closed in 2001.

Protection Agency. The wildlife habitat at Fresh Kills is in the process of being restored, but pollution at the site will remain for many years to come.

Making Cleaner Landfills

As the environmental hazards of landfills became clear, engineers started designing new landfills to solve some of their pollution problems. A modern landfill is not intended to be a normal environment where waste will decompose quickly because it is

A technician adds a liner to a landfill to prevent liquids from leaking into the ground, while another (inset) checks pipes designed to capture methane gas.

exposed to water and oxygen. Instead, it is designed to function as a tightly sealed container. The garbage is intended to be kept separate from its surroundings, thereby limiting the amount of leachate a landfill produces.

Modern landfills have systems for collecting rainwater and channeling it away from the garbage. Thick plastic liners cover the ground below the garbage to prevent liquids from seeping into the soil and water beneath the landfill. Leachate is collected and pumped through pipes to treatment plants, where many of its hazardous chemicals are removed.

Landfill engineers also work to control **methane** gas, another dangerous by-product of decomposing garbage. Methane explodes easily and is known to

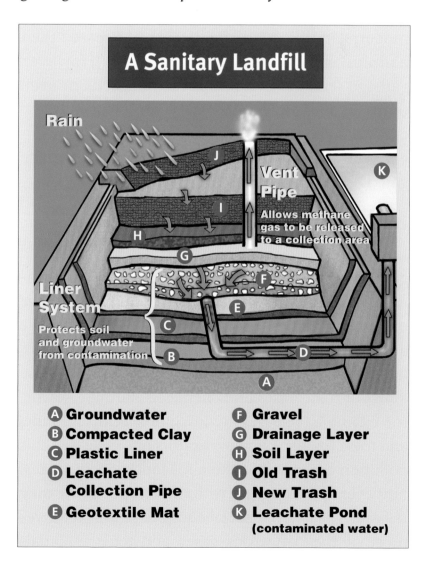

A Sanitary Landfill

Rain

Vent Pipe
Allows methane gas to be released to a collection area

K

J

I

H

G

F

E

Liner System
Protects soil and groundwater from contamination

C

B

D

A

Ⓐ Groundwater
Ⓑ Compacted Clay
Ⓒ Plastic Liner
Ⓓ Leachate Collection Pipe
Ⓔ Geotextile Mat
Ⓕ Gravel
Ⓖ Drainage Layer
Ⓗ Soil Layer
Ⓘ Old Trash
Ⓙ New Trash
Ⓚ Leachate Pond (contaminated water)

carry cancer-causing chemicals and contribute to the gradual warming of the Earth's atmosphere. Pipes buried throughout a landfill capture the methane. The collected gas is either burned or sold as an energy source. The methane captured from the Fresh Kills Landfill supplies power for fourteen thousand New York homes.

The safety measures engineers have taken in modern landfills have significantly decreased their harmful effects on the environment. However, garbage remains in landfills for hundreds or even thousands of years after they are closed. Many experts believe that landfills' protective plastic liners will crack and leak over time, allowing the garbage to contaminate the environment.

Burning Garbage

Landfills receive about 55 percent of household garbage. Another 15 percent is burned in large furnaces called **incinerators**. Although burning garbage may seem like a good way to get rid of large amounts of trash, this process causes other problems. When burned, the materials in garbage release a mix of toxic gases and chemicals. Burning plastic, for example, releases hydrochloric acid, chlorine, and toxic metals. Old incinerators once released this pollution directly into the air. Modern incinerators, however, are designed to limit the pollution they release. They have special equipment that removes most of the dangerous gases and toxic materials

Older incinerators like this one produced harmful chemicals and gases as they burned trash. Today's incinerators release far less pollution into the air.

from the smoke before it escapes through the incinerator's smokestack.

One benefit of burning garbage is that the fire may be used to create energy in a process called **waste to energy** (WTE). As the trash burns, it heats water in a boiler, creating steam. The steam turns huge turbines to produce electricity. One large incinerator can produce enough electricity to provide power for 50,000 homes.

The WTE process does not get rid of garbage completely. After burning, about 25 percent of the trash's original weight remains in the form of ash, which still needs to be buried in a landfill. This ash may contain some of the toxic materials from the garbage. As technology improves, engineers hope to find ways to further decrease the pollution created by incinerators so they can be more widely used to dispose of garbage in a way that is less harmful to the environment.

Transporting Trash

To meet the EPA's strict rules for controlling pollution, both incinerators and landfills are very expensive to build. WTE incinerators may cost up to $120 million each; landfills cost up to $500,000 per acre to build. This high cost limits the number of new facilities where garbage can be taken. However, most new landfills are very large and can take garbage collected from a wide area.

Many cities now pay large amounts of money to have their trash hauled to faraway landfills, often in neighboring states. Transporting all that trash in garbage trucks and tractor-trailers has a significant impact on the environment by using fuel and creating pollution. For example, since the closing of Fresh Kills Landfill, almost all of New York City's garbage is carried by trucks to out-of-state landfills and incinerators. Moving that much garbage requires 450 trucks traveling a total of 135,000 miles (217,000km) every day. During their daily travels, these trucks burn 33,700 gallons

A barge loaded with garbage floats past the Statue of Liberty in New York. Many cities, including New York, transport their garbage to distant landfills.

(128,000l) of fuel. The exhaust from these trucks is thought to add significantly to the pollution in areas around the city.

It is clear that despite the advances made in reducing the impact of garbage on the environment, challenges remain. Most experts agree that the key to solving the world's garbage problems is to cut down on the amount of waste that winds up in the trash can.

chapter three

Is Recycling Effective?

One way to reduce the amount of garbage put in landfills and incinerators is by **recycling**. Recycling is a process that creates new products out of waste materials. Approximately 30 percent of U. S. garbage, or 72 million tons (65 million metric tons), is recycled each year. Most experts believe that recycling is a good way to save natural resources and decrease the pollution associated with garbage. However, some questions remain about the impact recycling can have on decreasing the environmental problems of garbage.

Increasing the Rate of Recycling

In order for recycling to make an even bigger dent in the amount of garbage thrown away, more

Which Kinds of Plastic Are Recyclable?

Symbol on Container or Product	Common Uses	After Recycling, Can Become . . .
1 PETE	Soda and water bottles	Fiber for carpets, blankets, and stuffing for sleeping bags; also for new, nonfood PETE bottles
2 HDPE	Milk, juice, and water jugs; shampoo and laundry detergent containers	Nonfood containers or products such as motor oil bottles, trash cans, pipes, pails, and traffic cones
3 V	Vegetable oil bottles, vinyl construction materials, garden hoses, and shower curtains	Not usually accepted in home recycling programs
4 LDPE	Disposable cellophane wrap and diapers	Not usually accepted in home recycling programs
5 PP	Margarine and dairy tubs, pipes, and tubes	Auto parts, pipes, patio furniture, carpets, and toothbrushes
6 PS	Egg cartons, foam cups, and take-out food containers	License plate frames, home insulation
7 OTHER	Various bottles	Rarely recycled

An environmentally friendly garden makes attractive use of recycled pots.

recyclable materials need to be taken out of the trash. There are more than 8,000 programs across the United States that allow people to sort commonly recycled materials, such as paper, glass, plastic, and metal, and leave them at the curb for collection. As a result, 84 percent of Americans now have easy access to recycling facilities. However, even though many people participate in recycling, recycling rates are not increasing.

The reason for this is that most easily recycled materials are already being recycled. However, many other types of garbage—nearly 60 percent of materials currently thrown away—could also be recycled. These materials include food waste, electronic products, small appliances, and wood. Some cities have developed special programs to meet the challenge of recycling these materials. In 2003, Seattle's Solid Waste Division teamed up with electronics stores to collect televisions and computer monitors for recycling. In two years, this program kept 60,000 computer monitors, 37,000 computers, and 7,200 televisions out of local landfills. In 2006, California banned all e-waste from landfills, passing laws requiring electronics to be recycled instead.

San Francisco has one of the most far-reaching recycling programs in the country. The city's goal is to reduce its garbage output by 75 percent by 2010. To help reach this target, the city collects food waste from homes and businesses to recycle it using a process known as **composting**. It also collects and recycles large items such as mattresses, appliances, and electronics. As a result, San Francisco has already reduced its waste by 52 percent.

The Market for Recycled Materials

Increasing recycling to this level, however, can be expensive. Cities must pay to transport the materials to recycling facilities, where they are taken apart or processed. Sometimes these materials can be sold for a profit, but other times cities must pay recyclers to take the materials. The value of recyclable materials varies. Some materials, such as aluminum, have a high value because it is easy and inexpensive to recycle them and there is a strong demand for them. Other materials, such as plastics, have a lower value. Plastic is difficult to recycle because many varieties are often mixed together and have to be sorted by hand. Not all types of plastic can be recycled. If one piece of the wrong kind becomes mixed in a load, it may all have to be discarded.

Recyclable materials would be worth more if there were a greater demand for recycled products. Although people show strong support for recycling, they still make little effort to buy recycled products. Some people believe that recycled products are of low quality. Sometimes recycled products cost more than people are willing to pay. The manufacturers of recycled products are working to find ways to overcome these attitudes to make recycling more profitable.

Although cities and garbage companies that recycle can sometimes make a profit, recycling often costs more than dumping the garbage into a landfill. Still, most city governments working to increase recycling rates believe recycling's environmental benefits are worth the extra cost.

Recycling and Resource Use

Although it reduces the amount of trash sent to landfills, recycling does have an impact on the environment. Creating new products from old materials requires a manufacturing process that uses energy, water, and chemicals. Therefore, the recycling process also uses resources and creates pollution. However, supporters of recycling claim that recycling saves natural resources and reduces pollution when compared to making products from new materials. Most studies conducted by the government and natural resource experts support this viewpoint.

Where Does Our Trash Go?

In one year, the U.S. generates about 229 million tons of trash. That is 4.4 pounds of trash per person per day! Where does it all go?

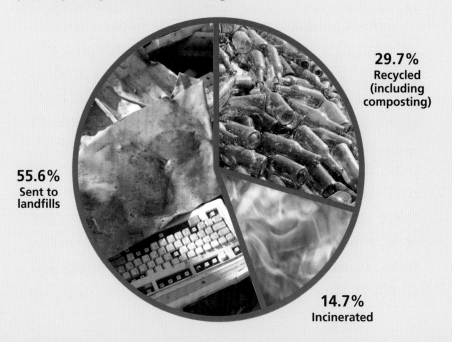

55.6%
Sent to landfills

29.7%
Recycled (including composting)

14.7%
Incinerated

Encouraging consumers to reuse paper bags (inset) is one way to reduce the amount of paper being recycled (above).

The manufacturing process of paper provides an example of the difference in resource use and pollution between recycling and making a product from new materials. When paper is made from trees, it requires lots of energy and hundreds of chemicals, some of them highly toxic. The paper-making process produces thousands of gallons of toxic wastewater and creates air pollution. It also takes large amounts of energy to fuel the construction of logging roads and to cut and haul the trees. It also takes trees—seventeen for every ton of paper manufactured.

Recycling waste paper into a usable product also takes thousands of gallons of water. However, far fewer chemicals are required and most are nontoxic. Compared to making paper from trees, paper recycling produces 75 percent less air pollution. It also preserves trees. In 2002, Americans recycled nearly 48 million tons (44 million metric tons) of paper, saving more than 800 million trees. Paper, however, cannot be recycled over and over. Eventually, the fibers in the paper break down so it cannot be reused and must be disposed of in a landfill.

Aluminum, by contrast, can be recycled over and over. Producing new aluminum from the mineral bauxite requires large amounts of energy for mining and manufacturing. Recycling aluminum uses 95 percent less energy. Recycling other metals, such as scrap steel from food cans, automobiles, and appliances, also pays off in huge energy and pollution savings.

Recycling Critics

Some critics of recycling argue that it does not really result in such large pollution and natural resource savings. When the energy used in transporting the materials is factored in, they argue, the pollution and energy savings are greatly reduced. Collecting recyclables requires extra garbage trucks moving through neighborhoods to pick up materials and take them to processing centers. These trucks use gasoline and create pollution.

Critics of recycling also point out that the materials used to make some products are **renewable resources** and therefore not in danger of disappearing. For example, many trees that are made into paper are grown on tree farms that are replanted after harvest.

Delaying the Impact of Garbage

Critics believe that recycling is not the answer to the growing amount of trash produced by **consumers** and businesses. Instead of providing long-term benefits to the environment, they feel that recycling only lengthens the time it takes for a product to be thrown away. Although recycling increases the life span of a product, those products will not last forever. Recycling opponents argue that most bottles, cans, and other recycled products will eventually be thrown in the trash. In the end, they will still end up buried in a landfill.

Critics also worry that recycling causes people to turn away from the more serious issue of how much waste is created. Because people feel good about recycling, they often ignore the fact that they are still throwing something away. A better approach, recycling opponents insist, is reducing consumption. On this point, nearly everyone agrees.

Chapter Four

Reducing Garbage

Most experts agree that finding better ways to recycle or dispose of garbage is only part of the solution to the garbage problem. Many communities are now focusing their efforts on finding ways to reduce the amount of garbage they produce. Cutting down on trash not only saves money, it also lessens the environmental problems of garbage transportation and disposal.

Source Reduction

Creating less waste is known as **source reduction**. Source reduction is the practice of designing, manufacturing, and using products in ways that minimize the amount of trash they produce. Both businesses and individual consumers can practice

A large container holds old tires that will be recycled. Used tires can also be retreaded instead of discarded.

source reduction. The first step is to ask questions about a product such as: Is it needed? Can it be made with fewer resources? Can its impact on the environment be reduced?

Sometimes the answers to these questions will show that new products do not need to be purchased at all. For example, a business needing new tires for its fleet of trucks may choose to have new rubber added to the old tires—a process known as retreading. Retreading has the same result as buying new tires, but is less expensive and creates less waste.

Because source reduction requires that fewer new products be made, it benefits the environment by conserving natural resources. Manufacturing and throwing away fewer products saves raw materials and energy. Source reduction also seeks ways to make products that are made to be more environmentally friendly. For example, using rechargeable batteries keeps the toxic chemicals found in regular batteries out of landfills.

Reducing Waste Through Technology

There are many ways that source reduction can be used to save resources and energy. One way is through the development of new technologies that make materials lighter, stronger, or less toxic. These products require fewer materials to manufacture and less energy to transport, and are less hazardous. For example, manufacturers have discovered ways to reduce the weight of metal cans and plastic bottles commonly used for packaging food and beverages. Since 1977, the weight of two-liter soft drink bottles has been reduced 25 percent—from 2.4 ounces (68g) to 1.8 ounces (51g). Aluminum cans are now 22 percent lighter, and steel cans have lost 40 percent of their weight.

The computer industry has also been using technology to tackle e-waste. An organization called the North American Pollution Prevention Partnership is working with electronics manufacturers in the United States, Canada, and Mexico to design computers and other electronics that contain fewer toxic materials. The European Union already has laws in place that require the electronics industry to find environmentally friendly alternatives to toxins in their products.

Reducing Waste as a Consumer

Not all manufacturers are concerned with reducing the waste associated with their products. Many products are wrapped in multiple layers of plastic and cardboard. Often this extra packaging is there for convenience or to attract a consumer's attention and adds no benefit to the product. Avoiding products with excessive packaging is a simple step consumers can take to reduce their own waste. Purchasing products based on their impact on the environment is sometimes called **precycling**. To precycle is to make shopping choices that reduce waste and make recycling easier. If enough consumers precycle by refusing to buy overpackaged products, manufacturers may change their packaging practices.

One easy way to greatly reduce trash from packaging is buying products in large quantities, a practice known as buying in bulk. Bulk products, often sold at warehouse stores, create less trash because many items are included in a single package instead of being packaged individually. Other shopping habits to reduce garbage include avoiding individually wrapped food products, and sharing products such as magazines and books.

Another way to reduce trash is to buy durable, or long-lasting, products. Using a mug, cloth napkins, and cloth shopping bags eliminates single-use disposable cups, paper napkins, and plastic bags.

In addition to feeling good about making choices that benefit the environment, consumers who precycle often save money. Many products with little packaging, especially items sold in bulk, are much less expensive than their overpackaged

Using cloth shopping bags like these cuts down on garbage by reducing the need for plastic bags.

Composting uses food scraps and yard clippings to make fertilizer for garden soil.

counterparts. Moreover, in many communities, residents must pay for each garbage can they set out for disposal. So when households reduce their trash output, they pay less.

Composting

Another easy way to cut down on household waste is by composting. Composting is a natural method of recycling organic materials such as yard trimmings and food waste. Composting has been used for centuries to decompose waste on farms, but is now becoming popular in suburbs and cities. People can create simple compost piles in their backyards by layering grass clippings, leaves, and food scraps. After a few months, the pile decomposes to form a material rich in nutrients that can be used to feed garden soil.

Some cities are experimenting with composting on a much larger scale. Many cities now collect yard waste separately from trash. These tree trimmings, leaves, and weeds are taken to composting facilities where they decompose in huge piles. Composting can make a significant impact on reducing trash. San Francisco cut its garbage by 15 percent simply by composting food waste from restaurants, homes, and apartment buildings. Another benefit to composting is that compost can be sold to gardeners. The profits from compost sales can be used to pay for the cost of composting.

Reducing Waste Through Reuse

Sometimes reducing waste can be as simple as repairing broken items or finding new uses for items that are no longer wanted or needed. Donating goods and clothing to charity is an alternative to throwing them away. There are more than six thousand centers in the United States, including those of Goodwill and the Salvation Army, that accept items to distribute for reuse.

The Internet has also become a valuable tool for finding new homes for unwanted items. Several Web sites specialize in helping people connect to exchange items they no longer need. One of the most successful sites is craigslist.com, an online classified ad service that helps people sell or trade goods within their own communities. More than 10 million people worldwide use craigslist.com each month. Another growing site is Freecycle, an online network that helps people give away items

In the future, e-books like this prototype may replace paper books, conserving landfill space, trees, and energy.

they would otherwise throw away. With more than a million members in fifty countries, Freecycle is estimated to prevent 50 tons (45 metric tons) of garbage from going to landfills daily.

The Future of Waste Reduction

Technology such as the Internet may soon play an even larger part in reducing waste. New technologies may change products in ways unimaginable in the last century. One such advance is the creation of electronic books. Instead of being printed on paper, e-books hold the text of hundreds of books, magazines, and newspapers downloaded from the Internet. All of this information is contained in a miniature computer that fits in the palm of a hand. Widespread use of e-books would save space in landfills, countless trees, and the energy required to make paper.

Creative ideas such as e-books may prove to be a valuable step toward solving the world's garbage problem. However, the most important progress will be made when people are concerned enough to make choices with the environment in mind. Communities, businesses, and individuals all have the power to change their habits and leave a lighter human footprint on the environment.

Glossary

composting: Heaping plant materials in a pile and allowing them to decay.

consumers: People who buy and use products.

decompose: To decay naturally.

disposable: Thrown away after use.

e-waste: Garbage made up of electronics equipment or its parts.

incinerators: Furnaces used to burn garbage at very high temperatures.

landfills: Places where garbage is disposed of in large amounts.

leachate: The toxic liquid that forms as water trickles through garbage and is contaminated.

methane: An explosive gas that is produced by decaying garbage.

pollution: Contamination of the natural environment as a result of human activities.

precycling: Purchasing products that reduce waste and make recycling easier.

recycling: A process through which waste materials are made into new products.

renewable resources: Natural resources that can be replaced after use.

source reduction: Cutting down on the amount of trash produced.

toxins: Substances that are harmful to the environment.

waste to energy: A process in which trash is burned in an incinerator, generating electricity.

For Further Exploration

Books

Mary Appelhof, *Worms Eat My Garbage*. Kalamazoo, MI: Flower, 1997. The author details the process for developing a worm-composting system to recycle food waste in the home or backyard, providing valuable garden compost and worms for fishing bait.

Rob Bowden, *Waste, Recycling, and Reuse: Our Impact on the Planet*. Austin, TX: Raintree Steck-Vaughn, 2002. This book takes a balanced look at different viewpoints about garbage issues. The author also presents thoughtful questions to guide readers in developing their own opinions on possible solutions to the garbage problem.

Eleanor J. Hall, *Recycling*. San Diego: KidHaven, 2005. This book examines the benefits and challenges of the recycling process. The author provides examples of the many products made from recycled materials.

Rosie Harlow and Sally Morgan, *Garbage and Recycling*. New York: Kingfisher, 1995. The book provides a hands-on approach to learning about garbage and recycling. Included are activities and experiments that the reader can conduct at home.

Web Sites

Earth 911 (www.earth911.org). Earth 911 provides resources on a wide variety of issues relating to improving the environment such as green shopping tips and a composting guide.

The Ocean Conservancy (www.oceanconservancy.org). The Ocean Conservancy's Web site contains information on trash found on the world's beaches and in the oceans. Visit the site to learn how to volunteer for annual Coastal Cleanup events or how to monitor beach trash in your community.

Rotten Truth About Garbage (www.astc.org/exhibitions/rotten/rthome.htm). This comprehensive site explores the many details of garbage. The site includes lots of information on making shopping choices that favor products that benefit the environment and reduce garbage.

Index